RELIGION IS DARKNESS

TUNJI OREYINGBO

ISBN 978-1-956001-01-3 (paperback)
ISBN 978-1-956001-02-0 (eBook)

Copyright © 2021 by Tunji Oreyingbo

All rights reserved. No part of this publication may be reproduced, distributed, or transmitted in any form or by any means, including photocopying, recording, or other electronic or mechanical methods without the prior written permission of the publisher.

Cover image by: Tunji Ishola

Printed in the United States of America

Contents

Dedication v
Acknowledgement vii
Foreword xi
Chapter 1: Introduction 1
Chapter 2: Religion 4
Chapter 3: Judaism, Christianity, and Islam 9
Chapter 4: Darkness Embedded In Religion 30
Chapter 5: Godliness 56
Chapter 6: Center Of Godliness 59
Chapter 7: Conclusion 76

DEDICATION

This work is dedicated to those who have lost their lives in whole or in part to various calamities that have resulted from the darkness infused by religion over the centuries.

Acknowledgement

I owe a great debt to many people who have been pillars of support to me. Their prayers, good wishes, financing, friendship, assistance, and guidance over the years cannot be over-emphasized. They are the stars whose leading and re-orientating light has contributed immensely to the writing of this book. Their true reward is with God, but I hope they will accept this little acknowledgment as my heartfelt appreciation. I would like to thank Dr. Joshua Yusuf and his wife, Janet Yusuf. I will equally like to thank Richard Odeleye and Sade Odeleye, Pastor Segun Odunuga and Sade Odunuga, Kayode Duroshola and Rita Duroshola, Kunle Ogundijo and Taiwo Ogundijo, Dr. Fred Eigbe and Dr. Itam Eigbe.

My joy knows no bound in expressing my cordial gratitude to the following people whose keen interest and encouragement was a great help towards the publication of this work: John Olanipekun, Fehintola Olanipekun, Pastor Funke Egbuedo, Sola Alabi, Tommy Oladimeji, Christopher Oladimeji, Toun King, Diran King, Olubayo Shode, Segun Ogunye, Olanrewaju

Ojelabi, Tajudeen Ojelabi, Adesola Oyebolu, Shina Akinbowale, and Chris Odijie.

I am deeply indebted to my respected teachers and other reputable individuals who have contributed to my spiritual journey. I wish to thank them for their invaluable help towards the quest for this work. I, therefore, would like to thank Pastor Mike Monsson, Pastor Tayo Ojajuni, Pastor Bunmi Ojajuni, Dr. Olugbenga Aina, Dr. Banjo Kale, Ayo Oyewole, Pastor Kunle O-Emmanuel, Pastor Folarin Akinsola, Pastor Tunji Ishola, Lara Ishola, Omoruyi Ogunsuyi, Reverend Folajimi Morenikeji, Tayo Adelaja, and my aunty Olasimbo Kale.

Several mentors, friends, colleagues, and family members generously read and critiqued certain portions of the manuscript, and many discussed specific portions with me. All of them made suggestions that influenced the final material. Among those who have read and commented on parts of the book or earlier manuscripts and whom I wish to appreciate for their labour are Pastor Femi Olawale, Dr. Olawale Oreyingbo, and Pastor Alan Carlson.

I thank my family for putting up with me over the period it has taken to bring this project to fruition, especially my wife, Solabomi Rachel Oreyingbo for tolerating my evasiveness, and always being encouraging and supportive.

Along the road, I came into contact with many remarkable people who gladly and generously gave their time and resources to this work. I want to thank these great minds, who stood with me in the journey towards this publication: Charles Nosa Osazuwa, and Dr. Oyemola Kale.

Above all, I thank God, the creator of heaven and earth, for his ever-present help. To him belong all glory, praise, and honour!

Foreword

This book is the result of my struggle to deeply understand who God is, his nature, attributes, and his expectations from human beings. It is my quest for creation, the enjoyment of life, and the gratification of after-life. In my search and research, I questioned my faith as well as other faiths and beliefs that I am aware of. I looked at the differences and similarities of the numerous religions and belief systems and later centered on the monotheistic religions. I became exposed through the Holy Spirit, to a deeper and more meaningful understanding of life and the after-life.

The purpose of this book is not to attack the tenets of religion, but to decide what we must give up, as well as what must be embraced for the sake of proper relationship with our creator. It thus becomes important for me to express that it is within the limits set by my experiences, research, and revelations that I have tried to scribble the best lines I could through this book.

If one can come to terms with the fact that all human beings are God's creation and thus connected to God in a way, it, therefore, implies that the more beneficial you are to His creature, the more He loves you. This invariably implies that the more destructive you are to His creature the less you are loved by Him. For God, is "love" and he wants us to extend love to one another. No wonder most world religions have somewhat similar versions of the "Golden Rule" – Thou shall love thy neighbour as thyself (Judaism – Leviticus 19:18); In everything, do to others what you would have them do to you (Christianity – Mathew 7:12); Repel evil with that which is best. And lo, he between whom and thyself was enmity will become as though he were a warm friend. (Islam – Quran 41:34).

This book recognizes religion and its benefits to mankind, as well as how it has relegated mankind. The book reveals some dark sides of religion, while harmonizing us with the center of Godliness – A figure that is revealed to us in all the monotheistic religions.

My hope in publishing this work is as simple as it is serious – that the Almighty God would use it as a tool to bring mankind into unity and full understanding of Godliness. Subsequently, human beings all over the world, regardless of our belief, will become Godly rather than a mere religious soul.

Chapter One

Introduction

Religions have been very powerful forces throughout history, across communities, tribes, ethnicities, countries, and even continents. They have sometimes worked for the benefit of humanity and at other times for our destruction. Religion has continuously inspired some of the greatest and most noble acts, and in the same sphere, some of the most heartless brutalities. Fundamental to all monotheistic religions as well as polytheistic ones, is, I believe, an inferred connection with the non-physical powers. These powers can be celestial, terrestrial, or chthonian, or a combination from the list. Therefore, human response to the experiences presumed through these connections, in thought and action is what constitutes a religion.

Religions are multi-faceted. They can be seen from many angles with the shapes too difficult for any one writer to see the whole. While there are mentions of other religions and sects, this book focuses more on the three major monotheistic religions of the world – Judaism, Christianity, and Islam.

Let me make it clear that the number one source of all our problems in the world and especially in the underdeveloped and developing nations is religion. Alongside earthly religious cohort come suppression, oppression, pride, corruption, envy, internal conflict, greed, selfishness, hatred, money-oriented charismatic drives, backbiting, man-centeredness, hate, man-idolizing, man-adoration, and canal mindedness.

The crusade of the middle Age alongside decades of conflicts, hostilities, persecutions, brutalities, and terrorisms between numerous religious groups who were expected to accommodate each other or live in peace with one another were all results of fuzzy religious mindsets.

What I have seen in the past few decades is that higher proportions of people are getting tired of religion. People in the world are no longer looking for religion. They are looking to secure their after-life. They want to achieve this by pleasing God, but many of us do not know how to please God. Religion has taught us that by pleasing God a person can secure a glorious after-life for his soul, but failed to teach the fact that it is not religion that guarantees the anticipated after-life. The truth is: we cannot please God through religion. It does not matter which religion anyone chooses to practice, whether it's Judaism, Christianity, Islam or any other monotheistic as well as polytheistic religions. The question, therefore, remains: How can we please God?

To answer this question, we will examine what religion is all about. Get exposed to the three major monotheistic religions. See how religion has infused darkness into our world. Take a good look at Godliness and how this differs from religion. Get exposed to the center of Godliness, and how embracing Godliness guarantees a secured after life augmented by a fruitful earthly living.

Chapter Two

Religion

Religion can be said to be the belief in supernatural being(s) and mystical agents, and the experiences associated with those beliefs. These experiences include such things as rituals, hierarchical structures, social alliances, rules, order, emotional experiences, as well as intuitive ones. Religion can be seen as membership in a group that is characterized by various beliefs and practices. Religious belief is a psychological concept, which refers to the attitudes people have in regards to the existence of supernatural entities. These supernatural agents are believed to be invisible. Some people postulate that they exist in realms beyond human beings, or that they are residents of places which are inaccessible to mortal beings. These agents often require sacrifices that can be ascetic in nature such as fasting, worship, abstinence from sex, abstinence from some food or drinks, prayer, praying procedures and modalities, body hygiene, and the likes. It can also be materialistically obligatory in the form of pilgrimages, tithes, animal sacrifices, monetary offerings, manual purchases, laity-to-clergy giving, temple maintenance, etc.

In a nutshell therefore, religion can be defined as a way human being tends to turn towards power(s) they presume are beyond the natural with the intention of finding meaning to the numerous uncertainties of life. Religion aims to give the required knowledge about the supernatural unto mankind, so that man can properly understand the universe, the purpose of existence, and gain some knowledge of the after-life.

Generally speaking, the major catalyst to religious belief and practices is fear. Major among the prevalent fears is the fear of death or the fear of after-life. These fears have been the anchor on which all religions rest. The "fear of death" ranges from the death of self to the death of associates, and in some instances, the death of those at arm's length. It spans the dying process itself, the loneliness of death, the pain associated with death, the personal extinction that may likely follow death and thoughts of the unknowns which characterizes after-life. It is no news to say that the belief in eternity is ingrained in nearly all world religions.

Religion is cross-culturally and historically ubiquitous. Religious beliefs have been core to human culture from time immemorial. This we know through archaeological proofs from ancient settlements in places like Egypt, Babylon, and some parts of Africa and Asia. These proofs evidenced strong religious rituals, and they are especially true when we evaluate events like burial practices. Ancient burial practices demonstrate belief in human post-death existence. It thus appears that religion has been substantial since the time of human existence. Furthermore, people have been made to believe in post-earthly existence over the ages through numerous facets and forms.

Religion defines how groups of people see themselves and how they see others. In most cases, people of similar religions see themselves as believers, while they see others as unbelievers. Common to all religions is the disapproval of their adherents' inter-mingling with the so-called unbelievers.

Religion is so powerful that it influences meaning and significance for groups of people. A person's religion shapes his belief and this belief defines how he sees the world. It dictates his behaviour and responses to other human beings. There is no doubt that culture, customs, and ethical values play an important role in religion. In most cases, people's principles, values, ideals, and cultures are commonly formed by the religion of their culture.

Religion aims to bring about the knowledge of God and other non-physical beings. It teaches and makes us aware of the existence of God and other supernatural beings, which can be celestial, terrestrial, or chthonian in nature. Such beings include but are not limited to the archangels, devil, angels, demons, trolls, gnomes, and spirits.

The three major monotheistic religions: Judaism, Christianity, and Islam have a traditionally held view that

RELIGION IS DARKNESS

God is one, and exists as a perfect being, with attributes which includes omniscience (all-knowing), omnipotent (all-powerful), omnipresence (infinite), omni-benevolence (morally perfect) and timelessness (eternal) among others. The polytheistic religions, on the other hand, believe in the worship of a pantheon or group of gods. The three major polytheistic religions are Hinduism, Buddhism, and Ethnic religions like the Chinese traditional religions as well as the African traditional religions. The monotheistic religions are similar to the polytheistic religions in the sense that they all have some kind of structured belief system. Each of these religions requires certain actions from its adherents which usually include some form of belief, worship, rituals, ethics, social behaviour, pious deeds, and some forms of regulated conduct.

Judaism, Christianity, and Islam are the widely practised monotheistic religions. These religions believe humanity is connected to one most superior eternal being. Judaism upholds that there is a single God who created the universe and has authority over all creatures. He is called YHWH, Elohim or Adonai. For the Christians – God is one – He exists in three forms: The Father, the Son, and the Holy Spirit. These three are one God, co-equal, co-eternal, with the same nature and attributes. Muslims affirm theistic sacred system in which Allah, the one and only God stands unique, distinct from, and superior to all created entities.

Judaism, Christianity, and Islam can be traced back to one iconic figure, Abraham. Abraham, who was formerly known as Abram, was the son of Terah. Abraham was the father of Ishmael, through Hagar. He was also the father of Isaac, through Sarah. Abraham had many children, but these two were the most historically significant. Their names will come up again in subsequent chapters of the book.

CHAPTER THREE

Judaism, Christianity, and Islam

Judaism

Judaism is a religion named after Judah, the fourth son of Israel. Judah is the dominating tribe of the southern kingdom and the predominantly surviving tribe after the numerous challenges, trials, and persecutions that the children of Israel had gone through. It is a national religion for the children of Israel. It is thus a system of beliefs and practices most prominent among the Jews. Judaism is a religion defined by ethical monotheism and Messianic hope. Abraham was the ancestral patriarch of the Jewish people. Isaac was the great-grand patriarch. Jacob, who later became Israel, was the grand patriarch, and the twelve sons of Jacob were the patriarchs. Though Abraham was the father of Judaism, Moses was the one who formalized the religion by bringing in a structure through the law and rules used to guide the co-existence of the children of Israel after they left Egypt for the land of Canaan. Thus, Moses is generally referred to as the law-giver and the laws are mostly called Mosaic laws.

Moses, the Law Giver

Moses was the son of Amram and Jochebed. Both his father and mother were from the tribe of Levi. According to Rabbinic Judaism, Moses was a prophet born at Goshen, Southern part of Egypt. Going by the Midrash, Moses was adopted by an Egyptian princess, identified as Queen Bithia. He lived between 1527 and 1407 BCE. Moses lived with his adopted mother in the palace from infancy until he was forty years old. At age forty, Moses ran away from Egypt when the ruling Pharaoh wanted him dead for killing an Egyptian in favour of an Israelite. Moses flew from the presence of Pharaoh and went to dwell in Midian where he spent another forty years. At Midian, Moses lived with Jethro, the priest of Midian, who had seven daughters. Jethro, who was also known as Reuel, gave Zipporah, one of his daughters to Moses as a wife. Moses was pleased to be married to Zipporah, together they had two sons: Gershom and Eliezer. His life was divided into three segments. The first forty years he spent as a prince in the palace of King Pharaoh, the second forty years as a refugee at Midian with Jethro, and the last forty years as the leader of the children of Israel. He was the man who led the children of Israel out of Egypt. According to the Torah, Moses died at the age of one hundred and twenty years. He was not sick, his eyes were not dim, and his natural force was not abated. He died in the land of Moab, and God himself orchestrated his burial in a valley in the land of Moab, over against Bethpeor, but no man knew the exact spot where Moses was buried. Moses was a prophet as well as the political leader of the Children of Israel. Under him, Israel was well organized and they practised what can be called theocracy.

Some Insights into Judaism

Abraham's grandson, Jacob, later became known as Israel. Thus, his children and future generations became known as the Israelites. They became known as Israelites from the time they moved to Egypt through the time they were settled in Canaan as a sovereign kingdom that had Saul as the first king. King David ruled the kingdom after King Saul. He ruled between 1010 BCE to 970 BCE. David's son, Solomon, became the king after his father. He built the first temple in the capital city of the kingdom, Jerusalem. This kingdom was further divided into two parts around 931 BCE – the northern kingdom retained the name "Israel", while the southern kingdom became "Judah". Around 722 BCE the Northern kingdom was destroyed and conquered by the Assyrians. Similarly, the Babylonians invaded the southern kingdom, destroyed the first temple and sent the war remnants into exile in Persia and Babylon around 598 BCE. It was while the Children of Israel were in Babylon that they began to be known as the Jews or Jewish people. A second temple was later built on the same spot where the first was built, but this was also destroyed by the Romans in 70 A.D. during the first Jewish-Roman war. It was the destruction of the second temple that made the Jewish people to shift their focus from worshipping in the temple to worshipping in local synagogues.

There are several sects or movements in Judaism. These include, but not limited to Orthodox Judaism, Ultra-Orthodox Judaism, Conservative Judaism, Re-constructionist Judaism, Reformed Judaism, Messianic Judaism, and Humanistic Judaism.

The Shabbat or Shabbath in Judaism is the seventh day of the week. It is recognized as a day of rest and prayer. It starts from sunset on Friday and continues until nightfall on Saturday.

TANAKH is the English translation of the Holy book used by those who practise Judaism. It was later formerly published by the Jewish Publication Society. Other popularly used sacred books in Judaism are the Mishna and the Talmud. TANAKH is an acronym or abbreviation of the Hebrew names for three divisions of books which formed the Judaism Holy books. Combinations of these books are what Christians refer to as the Old Testament. The three divisions are:

RELIGION IS DARKNESS

TA – Torah ("Law") – These are the first five books of the bible. They are referred to as the books of Moses. They include Genesis, Exodus, Leviticus, Numbers, and Deuteronomy. In Hebrew, the first five books are also called *Chumesh*, a word that is coined from the Hebrew word *Chamesh* (five). The Torah is commonly translated as "law", but it really means instruction. It contains 613 instructions, and the first of them is addressed to Adam and Eve: "Be fruitful and multiply, fill the earth and subdue it" (1:28). The books that make up the Torah were revealed to Moses around 1445 BCE.

NA – Neviim ("Prophets") – This comprises of two sections: The former and the later prophets. The former prophets are the books of Joshua, Judges, Samuel, and Kings. While the later prophets are the books of Isaiah, Jeremiah, Ezekiel, Hosea, Joel, Amos, Obadiah, Jonah, Micah, Nahum, Habakkuk, Zephaniah, Haggai, Zechariah, and Malachi.

KH – Ketuvim ("Writings") – This comprises the poetic books as well as other writings. It includes Psalms, Proverbs, Job, Songs of Solomon, Ruth, Lamentations, Ecclesiastes, Esther, Daniel, Ezra-Nehemiah, and Chronicles.

In Judaism, several important days are observed. Some of these are:

Passover – Is the last seven to eight days in the month of Nisan. It is to remember and celebrate the freedom of the Children of Israel from slavery in Egypt.

Yom Kippur – Is considered the holiest day in a Jewish year. It is a day spent in fasting and prayer.

Hanukah – Also known as the festival of lights. It is a commemoration of the rededication of the Jewish temple in Jerusalem after the Maccabees defeated the Syrians about 2100 years ago.

Purim – Celebration of life. To celebrate the event that is mentioned in the book of Esther, when Jewish people in Persia were saved from extinction.

Awe – The days of Awe is considered a period of repentance in Judaism.

Rosh Hashanah – Known as the Jewish New Year. It is a day of celebration of the birth of the universe and humanity.

Christianity

Christianity is a religion based on the life and teachings of Jesus of Nazareth, also known as Christ or the Messiah. Christianity began in the mid 1st century AD as a Jewish sect after the death and resurrection of Jesus Christ. What was earlier seen as a Jewish sect became an entirely different religion before the end of the 1st century. This development was championed by a prominent apostle – Apostle Paul. Apostle Paul, as well as the other twelve apostles, and their successors – the Church fathers, spread Jesus' teachings across Jerusalem, Syria, Rome, Egypt,

Ethiopia, and Asia. The adherents of Christianity believe that Jesus is the son of God, the Logos, and the savior of humanity. Christians believe that justification is by faith in Jesus as the Son of God and in his death, and resurrection. They believe that the death of Jesus Christ on the cross is a one-time sacrifice made to atone for the sins of mankind, and those who believe and profess Jesus as Lord will have a right relationship with God Almighty.

Abraham, the father of Isaac, the father of Jacob, the father of Judah, the father of Judaism is also seen as the father of Christianity. In the mid-first century AD, the Christians were seen as the people of "the way". They practised Judaism and were Torah observers. The only thing that set them apart from other Jews was their belief that Jesus was the expected Messiah. Saul of Tarsus also called Paul, who later became a prominent apostle in Christianity, was the man who redefined the new Judaist-Jesus (Jewish-Jesus) believers into a new religion that essentially broke away from Judaism. According to Paul, what mattered to God was not the observant of the Torah, but faith in Jesus. In his words, he says: *"Therefore we conclude that a man is justified by faith apart from the deeds of the law"* (Romans 3:28). While the new sect "people of the way" observe the Torah, but differ only in the belief that Jesus is the Messiah, they remain part of Judaism. But once Paul dismissed the Torah and any legal requirement demanded by Judaism, "people of the way" ceased from being a sect within Judaism, and became a separate religion – Christianity. This new religion became well acceptable to the non-Jews (Gentiles) such that between AD70 and AD100, Judaist-Jesus believers had waned in numbers and power, while Gentile-Jesus believers had waxed greater, making Christianity a predominantly non-Torah observant religion.

Paul, Apostle of Jesus Christ to the Gentiles

Paul was no doubt a pillar in Christianity. Most scholars do claim that he was the real inventor of Christianity though he had no intention of starting a new sect, neither did he plan to have any of his numerous epistles compiled into a book or have them become part of what is today called the New Testament.

Paul, a minister of Jesus Christ to the Gentiles, was a Jew, of the tribe of Benjamin. He was born as a Roman citizen, in Tarsus, the capital city of Cilicia. Saul was Paul's Jewish name, a name that could have been given to him on his 8th day, which was the day a Hebrew male child was usually named and circumcised (Genesis 17:12; Luke 1:59, 2:21). He may have been named after his father or a close relative or after the first King of Israel who was also from the tribe of Benjamin, like him. The actual year of Paul's birth is unknown but many Bible scholars have given a time frame of between 5 B.C.E. and 10 C.E. Udo Schnelle, uses the listing of the stages of life in *Philo*. He mentions that Paul described himself as an old man in Philemon 9, at which time he would have been about fifty-five years old since Philemon is presumed to have been written in 62 C.E.[1]

The Scripture does not provide a full description of the apostle's early life. His testimony that he was a Jew, son of a Pharisee (Philippians 3:5) provides an insight into his early life.

In the 1st century AD, the parents were considered the first teachers that a typical Jewish child would have. In Deuteronomy 6:4-7, God commanded the Israelites to diligently teach their children his commandments.

Having been born to Hebrew parents and with a Pharisee as a father, Paul would likely have started his unofficial education from home through observations. He would have learnt about God's commandments and the various festivals, feasts, ceremonies, celebrations, and symbols of the Jewish people such as the Passover meal, Feast of Pentecost, Feast of Tabernacles, festival of shelter, festival of lights, and the Day of Atonement. This part of his education would probably have been given by his mother and would have begun right from the time he was able to identify and differentiate things, at say, age two. This stage in Paul's life was very important because the feasts, festivals, and symbols were effective educational and devotional means of implanting a large portion of Israel's history in the hearts and minds of Jewish children from their earliest age.

---

[1] Udo Schnelle, *Apostle Paul His Life and Theology*. Trans. By M. Eugene Boring. (Grand Rapids, MI: Baker Academic, 2005), 57.

Going by the Jewish custom, the father would take the leading role in the training of a son[2], although education in a Jewish home for all children first began with the mother. Teaching in the area of spiritual matters was not the only responsibility of the father toward his son. Jewish education was also concerned with preparing the child to know how to live in the world. Thus, the father would instruct his son as well as teach him through his practical examples.

As soon as a child began to speak fluently, say between ages 3 to 5, his father would begin to teach him prayers, short scriptures, and make him memorize some quotes from the law and the prophets. He would ensure that his son attends the neighbourhood synagogue with him regularly.

Paul grew up in Tarsus, a city that was designated as the capital of the province of Cecilia in 67 BC by the Roman Empire. At around age 5, therefore, Paul would have been formally enrolled in an elementary school. These schools were attached to the synagogues. They maintained strict discipline, and their chief aim was the mastery of the Torah. Although the students studied reading, writing, arithmetic and some sciences, priority was given to reading, and every subject was treated in relation to the scriptures. By the time a son had graduated from this school, he knew the history and meaning of the Jewish customs and heritage and was usually able to quote nearly the entire Torah, as well as portions of the Old Testament books.

---

[2] William Barclay, *Educational Ideals in the Ancient World.* (Grand Rapids, MI: Baker Academic, 1974), 17.

RELIGION IS DARKNESS

Paul probably went to the Hillel rabbinic school in Jerusalem (Acts 22:3) for a more advanced study. One of the teaching methods at the rabbinic school was the use of memorization which was not limited to the scriptures but also incorporated the sayings of the sages. Other methods used include numerous repetitions, quiz, question and answer method, use of allegories, discussions, and debates. Paul most likely graduated as a Rabbi from this school, a step which later provided him with privileged access to the synagogues, and qualified him to teach in them.

The thorough instructions that Paul received in his Pharisaic Jewish home, the elementary school he attended along with his acquaintance with Greek customs while in Tarsus, as well as the rabbinic schooling in Jerusalem helped prepare him to become a great apostle. These stages of learning instilled in Paul a high level of discipline, vast knowledge of the scripture, and strong character building. Therefore, following his surrender to the call by Christ Jesus, and his seclusion in Arabia to ponder on his experience near Damascus (Acts 9:3-9), Paul stepped forth as a prepared soldier of the cross.

Paul was well-grounded and versed in the tenets and apologetics of Judaism as a religion. He was a Pharisee (Acts 26:4-5, 23:6), born of a Pharisee. As a Pharisee, Paul belonged to the Hebrew sect who saw themselves as people who are "separated unto YHWH" in the first century AD.

Paul was a Jew, but also a Roman citizen by birth. His family possessed Roman citizenship, which was an indication of his family's higher social status. As a Roman citizen, Paul had some advantages which later helped him in his apostolic work. He was able to travel easily within the Roman and non-Roman world. He was exempted from brutal methods of interrogation (Acts 22:24-29)[3], and he had the right to a fair trial when charged for any crime.

Paul was fluent in Greek and was equally proficient to speak the common Hebrew language of his time. Having schooled under Gamaliel, he would have been a person to reckon with among the elites of his time, no wonder he was likely known by face to the High Priest and the Sanhedrin (Acts 9:1-2). To wrap up his social status, Schnelle says "Paul was a city person: his urban socialization can be detected in his language and imagery".[4] In a similar fashion, I like to succumb that Paul was equally a low-level person when one considers his profession as a tentmaker – after the Damascus experience.

It is my understanding therefore that Paul was able to blend in at different social-economic levels based on his educational attainments and part-time profession. His Roman citizenship was also an act of providence in preparing him for the ministry he later received.

---

[3] John MacArthur, *The MACARTHUR Study Bible. New King James Version.* (Nashville: Thomas Nelson Inc., 1982), 1677. A commander who exerted brutal method of interrogation on a Roman citizen could end his military career or even cost such military official his life.

[4] Udo Schnelle, Trans M. Eugene Boring. *Apostle Paul His Life and Theology.* (Grand Rapids, MI: Baker Academic, 2005), 58.

RELIGION IS DARKNESS

The environment in which Paul grew, his educational achievement as well as the social status of his parents, without doubt, contributed to his self-image. Paul was an intense person before and after his conversion to Christianity. He was a strict adherent to the law and a man of integrity known as a person of exemplary behaviour from a very young age (Acts 26:4-5). Paul was proud to be a Jew (Acts 21:39, 22:3), a Roman citizen (Acts 22:23-29) and a fluent speaker and writer of Greek. All these contributed to his self-image as a person. Before his encounter with the resurrected Jesus at Damascus, Paul saw himself as a completely righteous man, for he had kept the law blamelessly. After the Damascus encounter, Paul believed that he, as well as the rest of the Pharisees, had misconstrued claims on what made one righteous before God. From then onwards, he perceived that – by the deeds of the law no flesh will be justified in God's sight (Romans 3:20). Paul came to the conclusion that only through faith in Jesus Christ can anyone be justified by God.

Christian tradition holds that Paul was beheaded in Rome as part of the order to execute Christians given by the Roman emperor, Emperor Nero. Apostle Paul died as a Christian martyr in a year between 64 AD and 67 AD.

Other insights into Christianity

There are three most important Christian holidays. These are:

Christmas – Celebration of the birth of Jesus.
Good Friday – Celebration of the day Jesus went on the cross to take away the sins of the world.
Easter – Commemoration of the resurrection of Jesus.

There are thousands of sects or movements in Christianity today. However, Christianity has two major early divisions – Eastern and Western theology. From these two major divisions came Catholics, Protestants, Orthodox, Assyrians, Restorationist, and numerous others.

The most holy day in a week to the Christians is the first day of the week. This is because Christian tradition holds that Jesus the Christ resurrected on the first day of the week – Sunday.

The New Testament is the number one holy book of the Christians. They, however, reference both the New and Old testaments of the bible, and see both as sources of religious law and moral guidance, giving precedence to the New Testament.

Islam

Islam is a religion introduced by Prophet Mohammed. Islam is an Arabic word that translates to submission. Islam, therefore, means total submission to the will of Allah. *Allah* is an Arabic word that means "the God", "the Supreme one". In a nutshell, Islam means a person's total submission to the will of God.

Quran is the number one Islamic holy book. The Muslims however, regard the Quran and the Hadith as sources of vital knowledge. The Hadith is the record of the traditions and sayings of the Prophet Mohammed. It is also revered and received as a major source of religious law and moral guidance. It is considered as second in authority to the Quran.

Abraham, the father of Ishmael is the father of Islam. Though, the revelations of Islam were revealed to Mohammed.

Mohammed, the prophet of Allah

Mohammed was born in Mecca in 570 CE into the tribe of Quraysh. His father's name was Abdullah, and his mother was Amina. Abdullah was a descendant of Ishmael, the son of Abraham. Ishmael's mother was Hagar. Abdullah, Mohammed's father was from a poor but noble background. He died while Mohammed was still in Amina's womb. Amina herself died when Mohammed was six years old. Mohammed was then cared for by his grandfather Abd al-Muttalib. After his grandfather died, his paternal uncle, Abu Talib took him in and raised him with his sons. Mohammed started working on a trade caravan that belonged to a wealthy older woman, Khadija. The caravan prospered under Mohammed, who was of an impressive character. Khadija proposed to Mohammed and they were married in the year 595 CE. At that time he was 25 years old, and his wife, Khadija, was 40 years old. They were happily married, had three sons and four daughters together.

After some years of married life, Mohammed began to meditate in a cave near Mecca. Islamic literature affirms that during one of his meditations, in 610 CE to be precise, he was visited by Angel Gabriel who ordered him to recite what became the first chapter of the Quran:

> In the name of Allah, the Gracious, the Merciful. Praise be to Allah, Lord of the Worlds. The Most Gracious, the Most Merciful. Master of the Day of Judgment. It is You we worship, and upon You we call for help. Guide us to the straight path. The path of those You have blessed, not of those against whom there is anger, nor of those who are misguided. (Quran 1:1-7)

RELIGION IS DARKNESS

Mohammed's key messages were:

1. The oneness of God, which implies a rejection of Mecca's polytheistic practises at that time.
2. The coming of a day of reckoning when all human beings would be held accountable for their deeds – whether good or bad.

After this first encounter with Angel Gabriel, Mohammed had numerous other encounters with the angel which was later documented in the Quran. Mohammed's message had positive reactions from the disadvantaged and attracted them to the new faith while it was met with hostility from the elites. This hostility later turned to persecution after the death of Khadija and Abu Talib in 619 CE. As a result of this persecution, in 622 CE, Mohammed moved to Medina with his new wives – Sawda, who was a widow at that time, and Aisha, who was the young daughter of his close friend, Abu Bakr. He also married Zaynab and had other wives. By the end of 629 CE, Islam was already dominating much of the Arabian Peninsula. This dominance was concretized after the conquest of Mecca by Mohammed in 630 CE. In 632 CE, a few months after Mohammed returned to Medina from Mecca, he fell ill and died. His death was after his return from what was termed the farewell pilgrimage. The farewell pilgrimage was the only Hajj pilgrimage that Mohammed participated in. During this pilgrimage, the adherent to Islam observed every move, gesture, and acts of Mohammed. Everything that he did became the typical Hajj precedent that has been followed by Muslims all over the world.

Mohammed was not only a Prophet but also a community leader, as well as a political leader. After Mohammed's demise, the successive early Islamic leaders were Abu Bakr, Umar, Uthman, and Ali. Mohammed along with these four successors, who ruled from 632 CE to 661 CE were models for religious conquest via action.

Other insights into Islam

Islam is built on five pillars. The first is the *Shahadah*. *Shahadah* is a witness to what the Quran asserts to be a primordial fact. *Shahadah* requires a person to bear witness. The witness is divided into two – the first is to assert the oneness of God, while the second is to affirm the apostleship of Mohammed and his messages. Thus, *Shahadah* simply means for one to bear witness that "there is no god, except God", and to bear witness that "Mohammed is the messenger (*rasul*) of God".

The second pillar of Islam is the *Salat*. *Salat* is the ritual of obligatory prayers. Salat is performed five times a day. During each prayer session, worshipers complete a circle of standing, bowing, standing, prostrating, kneeling, prostrating, and standing again. The *Salat* is obligatory for all Muslims, whether on a journey or in a state of war. The only people exempted from performing Salat are children below the age of reason, women during the menstrual period, and persons suffering from mental illness.

The third pillar of Islam is *Zakat*. The *Zakat* is an obligatory welfare tax to be paid annually on all surplus earnings. That is, on all their profits – for a businessman, or on all their income – for an employee. The tax is set at two and a half percent. This is to be given to the poor and the needy.

The fourth pillar of Islam is the *Ramadan* fasting. History has it that Prophet Mohammed was a man who observed a variety of voluntary fasting. The Prophet saw the Jewish community observing the fast of Yom Kippur, which he found to be a pious act of worship, and enjoined it upon the Muslims. The fasting of *Ramadam* was instituted in the second year of the *Hijrah*, after the battle of *Badr* which took place in the month of Ramadan of that year. Quran 2:183-185 stipulates the *Ramadan* fasting.

The fifth pillar of Islam is the *hajj*. *Hajj* is an obligatory pilgrimage to *Makkah*. It is expected to be undertaken by all Muslims at least once in their lifetime. It occurs during the official pilgrimage season. A ritual is enacted in four main parts: entering the state of consecration (*ihram*); circumambulation (*tawaf*) of the *kabah* and the running between the two hills of *al-Safa* and *al-Marwa*, journey to and standing on *Arafat* (the Mount of Mercy); and finally, the sacrificial offering of ram, lamb, goat, or camel (id al-adha). After the observance of these four steps, the pilgrimage ends. However, pilgrims often visit the Prophet's tomb in *Madinah* as well as other sites that bore witness to significant events and personalities of early Islam.

There are two most important Muslim holidays. These are:

Eid-Al-Fitr – is celebrated at the end of Ramadan, which is a month of fasting. The fasting takes place every day of the month of Ramadan during daylight hours.

Eid-Al-Adha – is called the festival of Sacrifice. It is the commemoration of the willingness of Abraham to follow Allah's command to sacrifice his son. Abraham did not end up sacrificing his son, for Allah grave him a ram to sacrifice in place of his son.

There are many sects and movements in Islam today. However, Muslims were earlier divided into two major branches – The Sunni Muslims, and the Shia Muslims. The Sunni Muslims form about eighty percent of the whole and it entails groups such as: Shafi, Maliki, Hanbali, Hanafi, Orthodox, Wahabi, Salafist, Barelvi, Deobandi, and some others. The Shia Muslims comprises the Ismaili, Twelvers, Alevi, Zaidi, and few others.

Muslims see Friday as the most blessed of all the days of the week. It is referred to as Jumu'ah, which means "to gather" –

the day of congregation – on Fridays, Muslims gather for prayer. They affirm that Adam was created on Friday. He was made to enter paradise on Friday, he was expelled from Paradise on Friday, and the last hour will take place on no other day than Friday.

Chapter Four

Darkness Embedded In Religion

Religion can be credited for lending meaning to human life through communal unity, which supposedly leads to brotherly love, at least for each sect. I tend to also agree that purpose can be provided through religion. Furthermore, when rightly presented and imbibed, Religion can be a medium for soothing people's fear of death and setting parameters for moral behaviour with postulations that punishment will be effected when those boundaries are broken. Religion can help to reduce or overcome the feelings of fear, hopelessness, loneliness, and guilt. It can also help to give meaning and purpose to life. These in several ways help inject self-control in people and most importantly help prevent suicide.

RELIGION IS DARKNESS

Religion has also been used to champion and forerun movements for peace, reconciliation, and justice. Such movements like the one led by the Reverend Martin Luther King II and his dream for America, the non-violent movement of Mahatma Gandhi in India, Mary Slessor's intervention in the infanticide of twins in some parts of Nigeria, Archbishop Desmond Tutu's movement against Apartheid in South Africa, and the 'Liberation theology' resolute of the South American Bishops against the corrupt dictators. Even at an Individual level, religion can be helpful. It can be a source of encouragement and many people find religious activities blissful.

As beneficial as religion is, it has twisted boundaries. There are no generally accepted boundaries across board in any religion. The issue is – some persons who claim to be Christians for example, are not accepted by the majority of that religion as being 'true' Christians. Many Pentecostals Christians believe the doctrines of Catholic Christians are unscriptural and may lead them to hell. Catholics believe Protestants are operating outside the true Church and may be bound for punishment in the afterlife. A similar scenario is apparent in all other world religions.

Religion also has its dark sides. These dark sides are as dark as darkness itself. Darkness is mysterious. It is terrorizing. It restrains us. It can be frightening or repellent. It can be an obscure place or can entrap us. Such is the case of Religion when it is devoid of Godliness. This statement is entirely true when one considers that countless people have been tortured, maimed and killed for religious reasons than for any other motive in the world. From history, one can learn that the torturing and massacring of people belonging to other religions by religious extremists have been prevalent. Below are some additional ways religion has negatively impacted mankind:

Religion and subjection

Religion is full of indoctrinations with the underlining aim of controlling the lives of others - the followers. Religion has become an instrument of oppression. It is worrisome to see well-educated people who are also easily fooled when religion is used to shield them from common reasoning. They obey their religious leader without asking any question even when not convinced. Without being forced, they willingly submit themselves to ridiculously dehumanizing experiences. Many geniuses who could have contributed immensely to the advancement of humanity have become myopic in their thinking and have suppressed their talents, and subsequently their contribution to the uplifting of mankind through viable inventions. Religious spirit is such that silences what God has spoken to you and how God is teaching you – it teaches that you follow the norms.

What more can be said in the area of religious brainwashing that has infiltrated our society? If one has not experienced family shattered by religion and its facets of man-made rules used to fool and programme their followers, then one cannot fully appreciate the need to put aside religion in favour of Godliness.

It is scary that some people are mind-chained in such a way that they cannot freely express themselves before their religious leaders. It is unimaginable to see the myopic ways in which many ardent followers think and act under the influence of religion and unwarranted overzealousness. Religious belief has altered the mind of an average middle-class fundamentalist to such an extent that he or she can kill and die "for God".

The TANAKH describes an incident which occurred while the Israelites were journeying from Egypt to Canaan, it says:

> Now the son of an Israelite woman, whose father was an Egyptian, went out among the children of Israel; and this Israelite woman's son and a man of Israel fought each other in the camp. And the Israelite woman's son blasphemed the name of the LORD and cursed; and so they brought him to Moses. (His mother's name was Shelomith the daughter of Dibri, of the tribe of Dan.) Then they put him in custody that the mind of the LORD might be shown to them. And the LORD spoke to Moses, saying, "Take outside the camp him

who has cursed; then let all who heard him lay their hands on his head, and let all the congregation stone him.

... Then Moses spoke to the children of Israel; and they took outside the camp him who had cursed, and stoned him with stones. So the children of Israel did as the LORD commanded Moses.

Leviticus 24:10-14, 23

Here was Moses – a man who undoubtedly hears from God. Faced King Pharaoh and demanded to have the Israelites freed from Egypt. By pointing his staff towards the red sea, the sea was divided into two and people walked on dry ground in the middle of the red sea while they had the two segments of the sea as walls on both sides. This is the same person that brought water out of the rock simply by hearing from God and obeying his instruction. So, Moses unquestionably hears from God.

Looking at the passage highlighted above therefore, how do we allow love to intermingle with justice especially when the life of other human being is at stake in an event? How can we prevent situations that can instigate human being to kill other human beings? Are we able to appeal to God and have His mercy prevail over justice? The people who reported the incident to Moses, what was their ulterior motive for reporting the incident? Could they have pressurized the process of Moses' hearing from God or influenced what he heard from God? Can we delay justice in situation like this or have God kill the person by himself rather than having other human being killed directly by us? All these are questions for a Godly soul to ponder on so that we are not just used as instruments to perpetuate other people's hidden agendas.

When religion comes to play there is the need to tread with caution. Religion is so powerful that it can be used to subject other people and make them do what they would not do ordinarily. Many religious leaders have used religion as a tool for getting their ulterior motives achieved by taking advantage of vulnerable followers. In the same spear, influential religious followers too have prevailed over religious leaders and used them to perpetuate ungodly acts. Whichever way we look at it, no man should have the right to kill another. Murder is murder! And murder is inconsistent with love. It is the highest level of hate!

Religion and Fear

Religious people are fearful people. In fact, the primary reason most of the religious people practice their religion is because of their fears. Prevalent among these fears is the fear of death. Other fears include the fear of uncertainties. In a situation of uncertainty, people tend to be more religious. Depressive economy, fear of losing one's job, a quest for material wealth, natural disasters, fear of being sick, fear of being involved in an accident, and such things as insecurities of life and properties play vital roles in how people turn to religion for refuge. Where physiological needs as well as safety needs are lacking, people tend to turn more to supernatural help and their agents for succour. For example, people in the third world nations tend to be more religious than those in the advanced nations for this singular reason.

The fear of potential eternal punishment in the after-life or the fear of not partaking in the pleasure that is presumed to be inherent in the after-life has made many to yield themselves to numerous religious abuses and manipulations.

Fear keeps us from getting what we want from life because opportunity, as it is said, lives on the other side of fear. We are therefore expected to cross the bridge of fear and arrive on the side of abundant opportunities.

Fear is not from God, it is from the devil. God empowers us! He enables us to love others sincerely and gives unto us a sound mind to live a successful and selfless life.

Religion and Deceits

The common phrase of an average religious person is: "it is God", "iinah Allah", and the likes. The very few that are rightly successful have been infiltrated with the common religious argot "it is God". Rather than using their success and achievement to encourage others on the need for planning, focus, discipline, hard work, perseverance, and deferred gratification, they will say: "it is God that did it". A religious hypocritical lingo that does not benefit the hearer!

Every matured Godly mind understands that God is the one who makes all things work together for good for those who loved Him. As such, what is expected from a successful person are words that will channel others who are coming behind on the path to tread. Not some religious verbiage that will do no good to the hearer, but rather make them a religious stooge that lacks the Godly knowledge required to profitably sow in order to reap abundantly. The principle that says those who plant in tears will reap in joy is the same one that admonishes us to plant our seed in the morning and keep busy all afternoon, for we do not know if profit will come from one activity or another – or maybe both. Many religious observers, for example, have become so twisted that they believe all you need to do in order to be materially successful is to regularly attend their worship place, pray, and be a tithe payer. They have forgotten that countless non-religious people are materially successful in a Godly way. This simply implies that success in life is not dependent on religion.

It is worrisome to see well educated individuals – professors, lawyers, engineers, doctors, politicians, business moguls, and some other professionals being made to believe that when you give money to a clergy or a temple, you are giving to God, and that what you give will come back to you in multiple fold. Giving to the temple or to the clergy is not a bad thing in itself, and should be encouraged. However, to get twisted that it is synonymous to giving to God has no scriptural backing. The monotheistic religious holy books only equate giving to the poor as giving to God. No more, no less! It simply means giving to those who has nothing to give to you in return.

Another common occurrence in the developing nations is to see some overly religious people term democracy as a representation of the sovereignty of the people rather than the sovereignty of God. As a result of this, they do not vote needless to say participate as a candidate in an election. Yet, they want a good government.

Leaders take whatever suits them from the religious books to con their followers and make them yield to their request. For example, Quran 4:74 has been used to manipulate many to commit terrorist acts. Deuteronomy 13:6-10 has been used to foster murderous acts. 2 Corinthians 6:14 has been used to destroy true love and valuable marriages:

> Let those fight in the way of God who sell the life of this world for the other. Whoever fights in the way of God, be he slain or be he victorious, on him we shall bestow a vast reward.
>
> (Quran 4:74 – Translated by International Committee for the Support of the Final Prophet)

RELIGION IS DARKNESS

If your brother, the son of your mother, your son or your daughter, the wife of your bosom, or your friend who is as your own soul, secretly entices you, saying, 'Let us go and serve other gods,' which you have not known, neither you nor your fathers, of the gods of the people which are all around you, near to you or far off from you, from one end of the earth to the other end of the earth, you shall not consent to him or listen to him, nor shall your eye pity him, nor shall you spare him or conceal him; but you shall surely kill him; your hand shall be first against him to put him to death, and afterward the hand of all the people. And you shall stone him with stones until he dies, because he sought to entice you away from the LORD your God, who brought you out of the land of Egypt, from the house of bondage.

> (TANAKH: Book of D'varim
> (Deuteronomy) 13:7-11)

Do not be unequally yoked together with unbelievers. For what fellowship has righteousness with lawlessness? And what communion has light with darkness?

> (2 Corinthians 6:14, NKJV)

Religion and Commerce

Religious commerce has kept religious organizations in the business for centuries. Sales of rosaries, religious manuals, oil, candles, incense, tesbih, fragrance, talisman, handkerchiefs, animals, and Halal food industries are a few among many. Before petroleum became the major source of income for nations, the Hajj was Saudi Arabia's biggest source of hard currency. Israel also made Jerusalem the centre of religious activities for Judaism and Christianity alike.

Most religious leaders – prevalent among African religious leaders - are plagued by greed – the slavery imposed by the economic system. They are driven by foundational materialism – the desire for an uncontrolled life of comfort and luxury. Greed has a dehumanizing effect. People who are controlled by greed usually see the need to achieve and acquire more as quickly as possible. Ironically, this passion makes their perpetrators feel discontented with what they already have and obsessed with what they do not yet have.

The TANAKH makes us understand that in the garden of Eden, Adam and Eve found themselves in the midst of plenty - they could eat from every tree, from every plant, and every animal except from one of the trees planted at the center of the garden – the tree of knowledge of good and evil. Despite being in the midst of plenty, they were discontented with what they had and obsessed with that which they did not have. They found reasons to see the fruit of the forbidden tree as healthy – good for food and they saw it as appealing – pleasing to the eyes, and a source of power – they thought it would make them wise. Despite having no restrictions on anything in the garden including the tree of life, Adam and Eve were derailed by just the one thing they did not have. This is the case with the religions of our time. Faith is balkanized by the most forefront religious leaders in their pursuit of material wealth, and this has infiltrated to their followers.

Most religious leaders of our time have become salesmen in the way they exert their followers, mesmerize, and manipulate them. Many use God's name to get their way. They use people up and throw them away. They capitalize on the love and honour the followers have for them to control them, and to keep them silent. They are more interested in pleasing their greed and never-ending demands for the pleasures of this world than doing what is right in God's eyes. They use God's name to get what they want from their followers. They water down God's word to entertain their congregants.

Many have become very proud and arrogant. Even those among them who appear to be humble are proud of their humility. They are like a lake that does not flow outside a boundary. Nearly all the money they raise from their religious establishment is spent on themselves, their worship building and empire expansion. They seldom disburse money for missions or to help strengthen the morals of the community and society they reside. The main thing their organization stands for is their pride and accomplishment. They believe success in the kingdom of God is equivalent to a headcount of their congregants and how rich and influential they are becoming. All that those who listen to them get is an hour to two hours of entertainment: exciting music, motivational speeches with few drops of scripture to mesmerize their audience and rouse the emotions of their fans. These ones are not Shepherds, but hirelings in Shepherd's skin. The New Testament says to the Good Shepherd "But you, O man of God, flee these things and pursue righteousness, godliness, faith, love, patience, gentleness. Fight the good fight of faith, lay hold on eternal life, to which you were also called and have confessed the good confession in the presence of many witnesses." 1Timothy 6:11-12

Religion and Corruption

The more religious a nation is, the more corrupt it is, and the more Godly a nation is, the less corrupt it is. Take a look around the world – the generally acclaimed religious countries are the ones who cannot take care of their people. They are the ones whose government cares less about the welfare of her citizens. Take any developing nation as an example. If you drive through the streets of a typical developing country, you will easily observe that the roads are bad, people are hungry and angry. Similarly, you will observe that there are thousands of churches and mosques along the road, yet bribery, kidnappings, rape, disorderliness, killings, embezzlements, and injustice are the order of the day. Political administrators at all levels rush to mosque on Fridays and churches on Sundays. They swiftly fly to hospitals in London, France, Spain, and Germany when they have any health issues. Yet, they do not think that it is a priority to have working hospitals in their own country. Is that normal?

In these same countries, the government spends huge amounts for people to go to Jerusalem and Mecca on pilgrimage without properly funding infrastructure and education. How can a nation develop without properly educating its citizens? How can businesses thrive where regular power supply is lacking? How has going to Jerusalem or Mecca helped any of the developing nation's economy? How has it made the people of any of these countries more Godly? The truth is – government has no business funding religious pilgrimage in any sensible society and developing nations should stop this in the interest of her people. Anyone that sees pilgrimage to Mecca or Jerusalem as a necessity should sponsor self! When we intersperse government with religion, corruption is inevitable.

In the third world countries, religion has been politicalized. Religious leaders have joined hands with the political leaders to enslave the citizens. This is evidenced in how they never utter a word against misrule in these nations. If they speak for the masses, politicians will stop donating money to their purse. These nations competitively build Temples, Churches, and Mosques while other nations are building technologies. Also, if religious leaders speak for the masses, they will not have the privilege to seek ungodly favour from the politicians and overturn justice when they feel it is required. Wickedness in the heart of most of those who claim to be close to God is disheartening, and this is evidenced by the way they live in affluence even in the midst of horrible poverty. In purely religious communities and nations, corrupt people in positions of authority whip up religious sentiments to evade interrogations as well as punishments.

If we take African nations as examples of developing nations, we see nations where government political leaders either claim to be a Christian or a Muslim, yet these nations still wallow in poverty while the children of each successive government leaders spend lavish money overseas. Go to government ministries and parastatals where the workers are either Muslim or Christian, you will be surprised at the level of bribery, laxity, and narrow-mindedness that prevails. If truly the monotheistic religions preach transparency and accountability, how come there is so much abuse of responsibilities by the adherents of Christianity and Islam? African nations have become godlessly religious to the extent that bribery is the norm in all professions and institutions. Yet, they claim to know God. Which God do they know? They continually ignore the words of Isiah in the Tanakh, and still, claim to be godly:

> Those who walk righteously and speak what is right, who reject gain from extortion and **keep**

> **their hands from accepting bribes**, who stop their ears against plots of murder and shut their eyes against contemplating evil - they are the ones who will dwell on the heights, whose refuge will be the mountain fortress. Their bread will be supplied, and water will not fail them. Isaiah 33:15-16 (NIV)

They claim to know God, but the truth is: many of them have been baptized by devilish immersion – greed and selfishness have taken a stronghold in their life. Corruption under the auspices of godless religion is killing developing nations, and this has to be ended if these nations will survive as nations.

Religion & Evil

No matter how we try to embellish it, intolerance to other faiths is intrinsic in every religious book. Religion has a way of uniting people of the same sect in massacre campaigns, with the perpetrators of such crimes seeing themselves as justified and guiltless.

Religion has been used to successfully tear human beings apart with segregation and condemnation. The Judaists don't like the Christians, and vice-versa. Christians and Muslims dislike each other, even though all these three monotheistic religions have Abraham as their patriarch. Even among the Christians,

Catholics are at loggerhead with Protestants, Protestants are not in good terms with evangelicals, and evangelicals and Pentecostals are contentious with one another. As if that is not enough, how do you come to terms with a Church group whose branches are secretly hostile to each other? Each clergy surreptitiously claiming superiority over the other and both cannot work together for the good of the Church group. Yet, each thinks he is not being canal. How can they demonstrate that they serve the same God and preach from the same bible? How can they lead people of sound minds?

Religious faith has successfully perpetuated inhumanity of human beings to other human beings over the centuries. Religion can be blamed for numerous wars of conquest, heights of abuses, and inhuman atrocities which human beings have committed against other human beings. In fact, Religion has been the most prolific source of violence in world history. Some of these acts of violence have been so brutal that people became callous enough to rip open other people's belly with the sword, many families, lineage, villages, and towns had been entirely wiped out. Young women stripped naked and raped in broad daylight, pregnant women's bellies slit open and innocent little children's brains blown away out of their skulls with guns, iron, rocks, and machetes. These happen repeatedly because two religious groups have different views about God. Their ungodly religious natures usually make them indifferent to the well-being of others.

RELIGION IS DARKNESS

People of the same religious belief see themselves as believers, and they see those who do not belong to their group as unbelievers. Most of the conflicts in the world today are a result of religious beliefs and differences. We see Christians against Judaists, Muslims against Christians and Judaists, Hindus against Muslims, Buddhists against Hindus, and so on.

During the Granada Massacre of December 1066, a Muslim mob stormed the royal palace of Granada killing more than a thousand Jewish families. The Spanish Expulsion of 1492 had the Spanish rulers declare that all Jews who refused to convert to Christianity would be expelled from Spain. During this expulsion, more than tens of thousands of people lost their lives trying to reach safety. The notoriously known Holocaust which spanned the period between 1933 and 1945 had the Nazis, who were predominantly Christians; murder more than six million Jews. In the early 1990s, the Hindu militants attacked Muslims with outrageous violence which is capped by burning their homes in Bombay and Gujarat. How many can we account for in the numerous on-going murderous tensions between the Judaist (Israel) and Muslims (Palestine) since 1948? What can we say about the March 2019 New Zealand mosque shooting which had about fifty worshippers killed? Or the April 2019 Sri Lanka Easter day suicide bombing that happened in three different Churches of the country and had about two hundred and fifty-eight people killed?

The sad stories of religious violence and brutality have extended over many centuries and across the continents.

Religion has often been a potent factor in the explosions of violence. From generations to generations, religion has been used to waste the blood and properties of sceptics. Most religious believers have seen it as justifiable to humiliate, fight, attack, destroy, kill, and annihilate the people presumed as "non-believers", including innocent little children.

Underneath the numerous violence and brutalities surrounding the extreme religious activities is the manipulations and blindfolding of the innocently adherent followers by the heretic leaders. For example, the Jonestown tragedy of November 18th, 1978 where a religious leader manipulated his followers into consuming poison, killing more than nine hundred members of the San-Francisco based religious group called "People's temple". How can we classify the Muslim terrorist leaders who use religion to blindfold and manipulate their followers into fulfilling personal obnoxious agenda? Phil Karber made us understand that:

> According to instruction manuals left behind, the 19 hijackers who attacked New York and Washington on 9/11 were exhorted to shave their body hair the night before. "Purify your head," it said. "Cleanse it from dross…Be cheerful, for you have only moments between

you and your eternity, after which a happy and satisfying life begins."[5]

In all, let us always remember that a conscienceless life has no reference to God, and in all cases, conscience demands courage. The courage to always do the right thing – What you will not wish for, do not do to others. Therefore, anyone who is not courageous enough to think, speak, or act in good conscience is not good enough for God, it does not matter whatsoever religion you practice.

Religious people are dangerous people.

In this section, I will share the experience of someone, who for the purpose of privacy, I will refer to as Brian. Brian was a Sunday school teacher in a Christian church. As part of their practice as Sunday school teachers in that Church, they would normally hold a meeting of all teachers on the first Sunday of every month after the Church service. The meeting would usually take about three to four hours. According to Brian, the number of Sunday school teachers at that time was about fifteen, they had a head-teacher who usually presided over the meetings. The teachers usually come to the review class after

---

[5] Karber Phil, *Fear and Faith in Paradise. Exploring Conflict & Religion in the Middle East.* Lanham, Maryland or Plymouth, United Kingdom: Rowman & Littlefield Publishers Inc., 2012): 6.

fasting throughout the day and would break their fast with some food and drinks after the review class at 6 pm. During the period of this meeting, they would review the Sunday school manuals, and ask biblical questions, or questions relating to life challenges. They would then try to answer each question raised to the best of their knowledge, while the head-teacher would enlighten them more and give a final verdict.

During one of their meetings, a fellow Sunday school teacher asked a question, and he said: "supposing I have five hundred dollars with me, which was intended for my tithe payment, but, on my way to Church on that day, I branched to see a brother whom I met sick. The sick brother was in need of five hundred dollars to take care of self. Is it right for me to give him the five hundred dollars I have or should I hold on to my five hundred dollars, bring it to church to be used for my tithe as originally intended?"

Many of the teachers who spoke on that day spoke against giving the money to the sick fellow. They argued that the money needed to be brought to the church to fulfill the tithing obligation. Two of the teachers argued that the money should be given to the sick person and the tithe for that period forfeited. After some moments of debate on the question, the head-teacher gave verbiage which supported the earlier view. He was of the opinion that "tithing is an obligation that every Christian must obey, irrespective of the circumstances we find ourselves". He argued that "God has a way of taking care of the sick and that is not any human's doing". He opined that "if everybody starts to give their tithe away, how would the church have enough to take care of her needs?" Therefore, he submitted that since the money was already earmarked for tithe, the onus is on the fellow to bring it to church as tithe and if he has any other money to give the sick brother, he can do so, but if not, God will heal the sick brother by his provident act.

How do we differentiate between Godly teaching and religious teaching? How can we rightly critic the message that is passed down to us? How can we ensure that we do not belong in the circle where religious obligation supersedes Godliness? How can we exempt ourselves from traditions of men that have over the years made us disobey the true understanding of God's commandments? What is the excess of fasting when the love for others has no place in us? Prophet Isaiah in the TANAKH was a man who understood Godliness in contrast to religion. He says:

> Is this not the fast that I have chosen: To loose the bonds of wickedness, to undo the heavy burdens, to let the oppressed go free, and that you break every yoke? *Is it* not to share your bread with the hungry, and that you bring to your house the poor who are cast out; when you see the naked, that you cover him, and not hide yourself from your own flesh? Then your light shall break forth like the morning, your healing shall spring forth speedily, And your righteousness shall go before you; The

glory of the LORD shall be your rear guard.
Then you shall call, and the LORD will answer;
you shall cry, and He will say, 'Here I *am.*'
(Isaiah 58:6-9 NKJV)

How do we develop our mind to a level where you don't just pray for a sick person, but take an extra step of sacrificing our time and finances for the wellbeing of the sick comrade or the fellow in need? How do we grow into loving our neighbors as ourselves? The answer to these questions is – Study and be bold! Study and meditate on the nature of God so that you can gradually be like him. Be bold enough to do the right thing at all times. Here are extracts from the New Testament teaching through some of God's messengers:

> But whoever has this world's goods, and sees his brother in need, and shuts up his heart from him, how does the love of God abide in him? My little children, let us not love in word or in tongue, but in deed and in truth.
> (1 John 3:17-18)

What does it profit, my brethren, if someone says he has faith but does not have works? Can faith save him? If a brother or sister is naked and destitute of daily food, and one of you says to them, "Depart in peace, be warmed and filled," but you do not give them the things which are needed for the body, what does it profit.

(James 2:14-16, NKJV)

In this scriptural extract, Apostle James taught Christians to be cognizant of other people's welfare, and not try to overlook or ignore the bodily need of others under the pretense of taking care of their spiritual needs. He says such spiritual display is unprofitable. Moreover, none of the Apostles taught us to tithe our income. Even Apostle James who was a fervent Judaist never admonished Christians to tithe on their income. I cannot remember reading anywhere in the bible that Christians are supposed to tithe. Where then did the twenty-first century Torah promulgating Christian leaders get this tithing rhythm which they chant and use to overturn God's New Testament principles about giving?

Though we are admonished by Apostle Paul to emulate the Berean Christians, it is a surprise that most Christians are similar to those in Thessalonica. Many do not crosscheck what their leaders tell them. Even when they crosscheck, they do with a closed mind. They are not open-hearted! As such they are neither a learner nor a receiver of scriptural revelations.

A religious person believes whatever he is told by his spiritual leader. It does not matter to him if what he was told aligns with godliness or not. He swallows it hook, line, and sinker. That is why a person can be told by his spiritual leader that his mother is a witch, and that person will from that point on neglect his mother in old age.

Religious people are dangerous people! A person becomes religiously dangerous when his presumed or assumed religious obligation usually cloud his sense of judgment. This inadvertently makes him an unpredictable instrument for perpetuating evil. It explains why we sometimes hear that a mentally fit person with a good future voluntarily bombs self and others in the name of religion. Thinking that by doing so he would be pleasing God, not knowing that his leaders had just brainwashed him to fulfill their own agenda. These are extreme cases! There are other things being done in the name of religion wherein the followers would think he is doing God's service, not knowing that all his presumed services are just to satisfy the ulterior motive of a leader, and has no eternal value.

Religious people believe that God operates in emotions. So, they believe that if they can just get God to feel sorry for them or to appreciate what they have done, then they can get everything they want. Unfortunately, God does not operate on the surface. He sees deep into the heart.

Purely, religious people are inconsiderate of others. They don't put themselves in other people's shoes. They neglect the pious portion of their holy book and never read their scripture with a mind to learn from God. They base their knowledge of

God on what their leaders teach or tell them. This singular act is one of the key factors that differentiate a religious person from a Godly person. A Godly person, on the other hand, studies the holy books of his faith to understand what God requires of him. He does not just take a portion of the scripture but goes through the entire scripture to have a good understanding of God and his faith. Not through what modern-day teachers have written, but directly through the major holy books – Tanakh, The New Testament, Quran. This is not to imply that reading other religious literature is not good. The point being raised here is that the Tanakh, the New Testament, and the Quran can be read directly and God is able to teach you without the use of other materials.

Chapter Five

Godliness

Godliness originates from the Greek word *ausebeia* which literally means the nature of being kind. It is a character and behaviour that emanates from the principle of genuine love for others. It is the outward behaviour that demonstrates an inherent reference for God in a person's heart. It is a personal attitude towards other mankind which results in actions that are pleasing to God. In a pious setting, no higher compliment can be paid to a person than for him to be called a godly person. A person might be a devoted worshipper, a conscientious parent, a dynamic preacher, a zealous temple worker, he might even be a religious guru, none of these things matter if he is not a godly person. The word godly and godliness appear about twenty-eight times in the New Testament, and six times in the TANAKH.

Godliness is not behaviour improvement, which is what we often strive for. Godliness is a deep change that comes from within, from God's truth being deeply implanted in our inner being. Unlike behaviour improvement that depends largely on personal willpower, the renewal of our mind is something that God alone can do – if we allow him.

God's grace teaches us to say 'No' to greed, selfishness, inhumanness, abuse of mankind, self-centeredness, corruption, bribe, waywardness, worldly passions, and materialism. It teaches us to live a self-controlled, upright, selfless, contented life, which translates to Godly living.

It is important to state that the display of spirituality or religious beliefs and conduct does not equate godliness. Those actions may not be motivated by the desire to please God. Godliness, in a nutshell, means conforming to the nature of God. It is the continual experiences of living a Godly life. It is an internal reformation which is reflected externally in a life that is cleansed of envy, hate, backbiting, greed, selfishness, injustice, embezzlement, bribe, fraud, covetousness, stealing, and such other things that are contrary to the nature of God. One whose actions and inactions originate purely out of love for all beings created in the image and likeness of God the almighty.

It thus becomes obvious that every human being is expected to pursue godliness. We are to pray for godly nature, we are to surrender ourselves to be godly. Godliness is not an optional spiritual luxury for a few people or groups of people. It is the duty of every human being especially those who profess to practice any of the monotheistic religions. This is simply because godliness has value in all things. It adds value to this present life and guarantees the abundant promises of the life to come.

Godliness is not external to the human soul. Rather it is an inherent power that lies dormant until activated by anyone created in the image of God. Activating this power requires proper spiritual diet, and discipline.

The fruit of Godliness is true love which is manifested by living for others. An important question that arises is: Can we put on the attributes of God without the dogmas of religion? I will say the answer is "Yes". There is someone whom the TANAKH, the New Testament, as well as the Quran point us to. This person demonstrated Godliness that is void of religion. He is the centre of Godliness.

Chapter Six

Center Of Godliness

Man has always been confronted with religious alternatives, worldviews, and ideologies. The question is whether there is a formula to discover which way to adopt. The debate cannot help us, neither can logic nor reason. The one thing that I have come to know – is to be enlightened in a godly manner. Like many, I retreated within myself in search of an answer to a question that was not easily available within the structures and institutions that surround mankind. In my quest for reason, hope, understanding, and the answer to this fundamentally oblivious question, I gained a deeper and insightful knowledge of someone who happens to be at the center of Godliness. He is a radical young Jewish theo-philosopher, who introduced a fresh idea that was uniquely unreligious, but fundamentally celestial.

Prophet Mohammed reveals the mind of God to us concerning him and says:

> When God said: O Jesus! Lo! I am making you die and taking you up to Me, and am cleansing you of those who disbelieve and **am setting those who follow you above those who disbelieve** until the Day of Resurrection. Then to Me you will (all) return, and I shall judge between you as to that wherein you used to differ. **As for those who disbelieve I will punish them with a severe punishment in the world and the Hereafter;** and they will have no helpers. **And as for those who believe and do good works, He will pay them their wages in full.** God loves not wrongdoers.
>
> Quran 3:55-57

And verily we gave Moses the Scripture and we caused a train of Messengers to follow after him, **and We gave to Jesus, son of Mary, clear proofs (like raising the dead and healing the sick, etc.), and We supported him with the holy Spirit.** Is it ever so, that when there comes to you (the Children of Israel) a Messenger (from God) with that which you yourself desire

RELIGION IS DARKNESS

> not, you grow arrogant, and some (of these Messengers) you disbelieve and some you slay?
>
> Quran 2:87

Concerning this unique figure, the New Testament says:

> Let it be known to you all, and to all the people of Israel, that by the name of Jesus Christ of Nazareth, whom you crucified, whom God raised from the dead, by Him this man stands here before you whole. This is the 'stone which was rejected by you builders, which has become the chief cornerstone.' **Nor is there salvation in any other, for there is no other name under heaven given among men by which we must be saved."**
>
> Acts 4: 10-12

And the TANAKH says:

> For unto us a Child is born, Unto us a Son is given; And the government will be upon His shoulder. And **His name will be called Wonderful, Counselor, Mighty God, Everlasting Father, Prince of Peace.**
>
> Isaiah 9:6

When Jesus was physically on earth, he was not a religious man. His theology, philosophy, psychology, and ideology far transcend religion. In fact, the religious leaders of his time saw him as a threat to their authority. They could not tolerate the way he questions their way of looking at things. This is simply because they were religious – He, was Godly.

Jesus is the link between the earth and heaven. In Jesus we see the creator himself coming into the world. The true light Himself descended from heaven in his entirely loving nature, illuminating the darkness that religion has introduced. He did this by revealing God to us and keeping us informed. No wonder Apostle John reveals to us that "God is light and in Him is no darkness at all"

In the Quran, we see how Prophet Mohammed has revealed to us the person of Jesus and his nature. We are able to deduce that this same Jesus is more than a prophet:

- The name Jesus appears thirty-four times in the Quran.
- Jesus is the word of God, He is the Messiah. (Quran 3:45-46)
- Jesus created life through the mud. Meaning he is able to give life. (Quran 5:110-111)
- Among every name mentioned in the Quran, only Jesus was mentioned to have been strengthened with

the Holy Spirit. This was mentioned three times in the Quran (2:87, 2:253, 5:110)
- Jesus was born by a virgin – Mary, was her name. (Quran 3:45-48)
- Jesus did several miracles, including raising the dead. (Quran 5: 110-111)
- This same Mary – the mother of Jesus, is the most prominent woman in the Quran. The Quran puts her in the position of highest honour among women, being the mother of the Messiah. In fact, chapter 19 of the Quran is titled: "Mary".
- Mary, the mother of Jesus was pure. That is, she was without any sin (Quran 3:42)

According to Apostle Paul in the New Testament literature, the crucifixion of Jesus has transcended the Jewish law. Meaning, the traditional observance of the law in the TANAKH – which used to make us righteous before God – has henceforth been replaced by faith in Christ alone – we shall be saved through Jesus Christ from the wrath of God (Romans 5:9). Not through Christianity! Not through Islam! Not through Judaism! And not through any other form of religion – be it monotheistic or polytheistic.

Jesus was born to a young Jewish virgin named Mary in the town of Bethlehem, located in the southern part of Jerusalem. Most historians believe that he was born between 7 BCE and 2

BCE. The New Testament, as well as the Quran teaches us that his conception was a supernatural event, with Mary becoming impregnated via the Holy Spirit. Very little is known about Jesus' childhood. The New Testament reveals that when he was a baby he was taken to Egypt and two years later he was brought back to Israel. His earthly father, Joseph, was a carpenter, of the tribe of Judah. Jesus grew up in Nazareth, was raised as Jewish, and according to most scholars, he aimed to reform Judaism, not create a new religion.

When he was around thirty years old, Jesus started his public ministry after being baptized in the Jordan River by the prophet known as "John the Baptist". For about three years, Jesus traveled with twelve appointed disciples, teaching large groups of people and performing what witnesses described as healing, signs, wonders, and miracles. Some of the most well-known miraculous events included the raising of dead people. Prominent among those raised from the dead was a man named Lazarus, who was dead for four days before Jesus raised him back to life. He also worked on the sea, healed the sick, the blind, the deaf, the dumb, those with several mental sicknesses and paralysis, turned water to wine, set the captives free, and delivered those who were religiously oppressed by the devil or by other men.

Many scholars believe Jesus died between 30 A.D. and 33 A.D. According to the New Testament, Jesus was arrested, tried and condemned to death by a Roman governor named

RELIGION IS DARKNESS

Pontius Pilate who issued the order to have Jesus killed after being pressured by Jewish leaders who alleged that Jesus was guilty of a variety of crimes, including blasphemy.

Jesus was crucified by Roman soldiers in Jerusalem, and his body was laid in a tomb. According to the New Testament, three days after his crucifixion, Jesus' body was missing. From that third day, up to fifty days after his death, more than five hundred people reported seeing him or having an encounter with him. Authors of the New Testament literature say that the resurrected Jesus ascended into Heaven afterward.

Some of the main themes that Jesus taught include:

- Love God.
- Love your neighbor as yourself.
- Forgive others who have wronged you.
- Love your enemies and pray for them.
- Ask God for the forgiveness of your sins, and forsake sins.
- That He is the Messiah and has the authority to forgive others.
- Repentance of sins is essential.
- Don't be hypocritical.
- Don't judge others.
- Give to those who ask from you.
- Be compassionate and merciful.

- The Kingdom of God is near, and all should repent their evil ways and reconcile with God.

The earthly Jesus was a man who would not yield to pressures of religious conformity. Jesus was a man whose teachings were most importantly revolutionary. He was never afraid to provoke those who suppressed the truth in an effort to enslave the masses with their religious bigotry. Jesus Christ was more than a prophet! He was more than a priest. He was a high priest of the very highest order. He represented God before mankind, and continually represents mankind before God. He was not only a king but a king of kings, with authority over all kings and kingdoms in the universe, beneath the universe and above the universe. Jesus Christ is the Messiah. The anointed one of God! He is the deliverer of mankind and our unique mediator. He came for the whole world, not just for the Christians, and still stands as the representative for those who trust in him.

Moses founded and promoted Judaism. He wrote the law. Paul was the founder and promoter of Christianity. He wrote more than half of the New Testament literature. Mohammed founded and promoted Islam. He authored the Quran. Jesus did not create a new religion neither did he write any religious book, though he was able to read and write. This demonstrated to us that he had not come to establish a religion or to make mankind more religious, but to reunite us with God by renewing our hearts. He was born a Jew, lived as a Jew, practised Judaism, and was buried as a Jew. It was however clear from his teachings that he came to redefine our relationship with God and turn us away from religion towards God – the creator of the universe. His mission was to deliver us from the darkness which religion has introduced and put us in the illuminating light entrenched in godliness. Here is what John says he said about himself:

> Then Jesus spoke to them again, saying, "I am the light of the world. He who follows Me shall not walk in darkness, but have the light of life."
>
> (John 8:12)
>
> Most assuredly, I say to you, he who hears My word and believes in Him who sent Me has everlasting life, and shall not come into judgment, but has passed from death into life.
> (John 5:24)

With the above, one is convinced that being in Jesus is a guarantee that your after-life is secured. No need to be afraid of your after-life anymore.

Jesus was not a religious person. Though he practised Judaism, here are some of his teachings which contradict Judaism's teachings:

- Jesus taught us that we show mercy to the wicked. He taught us to love our enemies (Mathew 5:38-48). This contradicts TANAKH which teaches to take an eye for an eye, a tooth for tooth, hand for hand, foot for foot, and life for life (Leviticus 24:17-22).
- Jesus taught that people can get to God only through him (John 14:6). This opposes what TANAKH teaches in Exodus 20:3, 34:14.
- Jesus has the power to forgive sins and he forgives sins (Mathew 9:6). This opposes what TANAKH teaches that the priest makes atonement for the people before God to cleanse them from their sins (Leviticus (16:23-30).

Jesus Christ did not intend to start a new religion or for those who believe in him to be a separate religious body. This is made evident in the fact that:

- Firstly, Jesus of Nazareth practised rabbinic Judaism while on earth.
- Secondly, his followers were part of Judaism before Paul's Torah-independent Gospel was introduced and became dominating.

RELIGION IS DARKNESS

- Thirdly, Jesus was able to read and write, but he never wrote any religious guidelines, rather he tried to correct the misconstrued beliefs in his religion.
- Fourthly, Jesus never tried to sell any religion. Rather he let mankind know that He is the way to God, He is the light of the world, He is the truth, and those who follow in his footsteps will be in God's good book.

The truth is: God does not care about how many times you read through the bible in a year, he does not care about how often you fast or pray, or go to the temple, or go on the mountain, or tithe on your income, or go on religious pilgrimage, or participate in any of the religious rituals. None of these things is bad in themselves, but the inward renewal that comes from God through the indwelling of Jesus Christ, the Holy One of God, is what God is yearning for. No wonder the psalmist, Robert Lowry in 1876, wrote:

> What can wash away my sin?
> Nothing but the blood of Jesus
> What can make me whole again?
> Nothing but the blood of Jesus
>
> Oh, precious is the flow
> That makes me white as snow
> No other fount I know
> Nothing but the blood of Jesus

God does not want us to work hard at trying to be good. He does not want you to go through the motions of religion – showing up at the temple for the sake of it, fasting to be seen as devout, praying publicly to be acknowledged by men, pretending to be someone you are not, or demonstrating our "proud full" humility. God wants the truth, sincere love for others, honesty, transparency, and presentation of your vulnerability. He wants you to lay your soul bare before him, to smash your pride in his presence, to place yourself completely in His able hands, so that he can refine, form, and shape you from inside out. God wants a heart that yearns for His indwelling. He wants a heart that sincerely loves others like themselves. What more can be said, but to put it in simple terms: Jesus of Nazareth is that one person that is worthy of emulation!

Good supplants Truth

There is an ancient story of a lawyer who asked a simple but theologically complex question. The question was directed to an ambassador from heaven. The lawyer asked – what must I do to inherit eternal life? This question is synonymous with – What shall I do to be saved? Or what do I need to do to partake in the anticipated eschatological blessing? Or how can I be sure I will partake of paradise? In other words, what must I do to please God? The question can be further simplified as – what does God require of me? To answer the question, the ambassador asked the lawyer: "How did you interpret the laws of God?" and he answered: "Thou shall love the Lord thy God with all thy heart, with all thy soul, with all thy strength, and with your entire mind; and thy neighbour as thyself." The ambassador answered: "Go and do this, and your ways will please God". The lawyer, however, wanted to justify himself, so he asked: "who is my neighbour?" To expound on who the neighbour is, the ambassador gave the story below:

There was a certain man who went down from Jerusalem to Jericho. During his journey, he fell among thieves, who stripped him of his belongings, wounded him, and left him half dead. By chance, a certain priest came down that road, but when he saw the wounded man, he passed by on the other side. Similarly, a religious worker came down the path, when he arrived at the place, came around, looked at the wounded man, and passed by on the other side. But a certain foreigner, who happened to be a Samaritan, as he journeyed, came where the wounded man was. When he saw the man, he had compassion on him. He went to him, bandaged his wounds, poured oil and wine on the wound, set him on his animal, brought him to an inn, and took care of him. On the next day, when he was to leave, he took out some money, gave them to the innkeeper, and said to him "Take care of him; and whatever more you spend, when I come again, I will repay you." The question then is: which of these three men do you think displayed Godliness to him who fell among the thieves? The answer to the question asked is not far-fetched. The truth is: the priest could be going to his temple at that early hour to lead the prayer, and possibly the religious worker too was going to his temple to organize worship. The foreigner too could be on his way to his temple or perhaps on a very important business trip. The ambassador from heaven concluded that whatsoever could have been the mission of these three people before meeting the wounded man becomes worthless when they ignored to shower love on the wounded. He thus reiterates that love for a fellow human is simply the summary of God's law. Love should not just be shown to people of similar faith as ours, but to all people, regardless of their religion, skin colour, race, language, tribe, gender or belief. Let love be without pretence, the ambassador taught. With this story, the narrator insists that the listeners must, on all occasions that call for it, do as the Samaritan had done to fulfil the commandments of God. To do as the Samaritan did requires an active concern for others, an act which ignores and transcends social as well as religious barriers. The ambassador's answer depicts that devotion to God is expressed by showing love to other humans. He used an adjective to qualify this particular Samaritan. He called him "good". He says, he was a good Samaritan. Not a nice Samaritan, but a good one. When we juxtapose this words with Jesus' statement according to Mark in the New Testament, that "no one is good except God alone" (Mark 10:18), then it becomes permissible to conclude that this particular Samaritan has demonstrated a topnotch attribute of God to be qualified as "good". Everybody who is truly human knows that the foreigner who showed mercy unto him who fell among robbers is the Godly person. The others were just religious. I, therefore, conclude that Godliness transcends religion just as good supplants truth.

To those who know God, their heart of compassion, conscience, and justice always align with the true and deep meaning of the word of God, and not its literal interpretations by those we have "gurualized" in our life.

Jesus is the correction of all the dark ideas and images we have about God. He experienced darkness on the cross so that those who live in him henceforth will not live in darkness. In the encounter with Jesus, we experience a fresh perspective of who God is, and what God desires of us.

Differences between Religion and Godliness

Category	Religion	Godliness
Self	Selfish and Greedy	Selfless and Contented
Passion	Promotes Empire building	Promotes the building up of human's mind
Relationship	Legalistic and judgemental of others	Tolerance and accommodating of others
Speeches	Instigates violence, crusades, oppression, and terrorism	Instigates love, care, and humanity
Effect	Divides humanity	Unites Mankind

Breed	Breeds hidden boasting	Breeds genuine humility
Value for life	Believe that only the life of those who practice the same religion with them is valuable.	Believe that human life has equal value notwithstanding the religion practised
Mindset	Believe that unbelievers should be killed or maltreated	Believe that unbelievers should be enlightened and well treated
Messages	Materialistic and earthly	Godly and Celestial
Way of Life	Full of Manipulations	Good and Truthfully Minded
Emotion	Fearful – Promotes fear	Faith-full – Promotes Love – the antidote to fear
Advancement	Promotes material acquisition	Promotes Godly progression
Favour	Favours the rich over the poor	No favouritism – Treats everyone equal
Pronouncements and Thoughts	Frequently mention God in their speeches but their thoughts are Godless. Isaiah 29:13	They don't frequently mention God in their speeches but believe in God with their hearts. Jeremiah 31:33

What Kind of Person Are You?

In this world, we only have two tribes - the good, and the bad. Religion does not matter, skin color does not matter, ethnicity does not matter, neither social status nor economic status matter in this context. The good people, as well as the bad, can come in any form. It can come from any tribe or any faith. If you are good, you are good, and if you are bad, you are bad.

A bad person can begin the journey towards good – that is, towards godliness by renewing his heart, and asking God daily for help.

It is not what we eat or drink that determines whether we are good or bad. It is not how we give to our temple or the place of worship, or the Guru in our life that depicts our association with God. Our relationship with God is reflected in our relationship to fellow human beings – Our thoughts, acts, speeches, way of life, and worldview go a long way to show to the world and heavens what kind of person we are.

Chapter Seven

Conclusion

When religion is the subject, there is a fundamental question that mankind has failed to ask. We have failed to ask this question from generation to generation. Every protagonist in every religion has failed to ask this foundational question. The question is such that it's supposed to come first to anyone who practices one religion or the other. It is a question that if one asks himself and answers genuinely, it has the tendency to open doors of enlightenment unto the soul that seeks such understanding. I recognize that for some of us this question never crosses our mind, and as a result, we never asked or meditated on it. For some, we had deliberately on several occasions, shy away from asking ourselves this very important question. And for some, we intentionally discard the question whenever it crosses our mind in one form or another.

RELIGION IS DARKNESS

This question is simple, but it's not easy. The question is: Is God a Judaist, a Christian, or a Muslim? This is just to pick a few of the exclusive monotheistic religions. Would you say that God is a "Judachristlam" – practices or belongs to all the above mentioned monotheistic religions, or would you subscribe to the idea that God does not practise or belong to any of the aforementioned religions? Is God a Polytheist? With your knowledge of God, how would you classify him? Which of the religions would you ascribe to him? Does he belong to all or does he belong to none?

The answer to this question is multi-faceted. It is justified to say that God is not in any of these religions. When one considers the height of violence and abuses that human beings had unleashed and still unleashes on other human beings in the name of religion, this statement is reasonable. It is even more disheartening when these evils are backed up with extracts from religious holy books. On the other hand, it is okay to say God belongs to all the religions when one considers the positive contributions human beings have made as a result of religious beliefs or through religious institutions. For instance, how do we place those who on moral grounds (acquired through religions and religious organizations) have challenged leaders, commanders, and even scriptures that are dehumanizing and against godly conscience?

Therefore, the onus to see God's presence or absence in any religion is on each one of us. We must all strive to balance the call to obey that which is good and godly and to disobey that which is bad and ungodly. This way we all can rescue our world from the excesses of misanthropes.

The bible is not a closed book, and so is any holy scripture. Therefore, religious books are not devoid of human reasoning and the application of godly moral conscience. Godliness will not allow evil to be called good, and it will not be seen to rejoice or celebrate tragic events as God's judgement upon people but rather stand in the gap for the victims.

It is forbidden for any truly religious adherent soul to compromise natural moral conscience in the name of obeying God or the written words in any of the holy books. If it does, such a religion is void of godliness, making it unprofitable to God, as well as to mankind. God is able to punish those he chooses to punish by himself and does not need mortal beings to destroy other human beings in the name of obeying God or doing his will.

The story of Korah, Dathan, Abiram, and On who rebelled against Moses and Aaron, along with that of Lot and the people of Sodom, which we learnt from Tanakh teach us that God is able to inflict punishment on those who fail to do his will by himself. In these stories, God wreaks his punishment without having any human being as an instrument for disseminating it. Meaning, God is able to judge and exert punishment on individuals or community by himself without the help of anyone. Therefore, the idea of using God's word to support our individual evil mindedness must stop. God is not evil!

We have also learnt from the same Tanakh, through Prophet Jonah and the people of Nineveh that God can choose to change his mind. The people of Nineveh repented of their sins and God revoked the pronounced punishment. Through the book of Jonah, we can learn that the heart of God is generously compassionate, and judgement should be left to him and him alone.

God is not Tanakh, He is not Bible, He is not the New Testament, and He is not Quran. God is different from the Holy books. He is over and above the Holy books, and transcends them all. God can be appealed to beyond the revelations of the Holy books. God's stand can be moved, and his words can be fine-tuned from all evilness. God is greater than every written religious literature. He is greater than the law, He is greater than the gospel, He is greater than the revelations giving to Mohammed. As we have seen from the Tanakh, God can pronounce punishment and have it revoked. It thus proves to us that God is the one to fear and not what was written about him. Sometimes, therefore, for God's sake, and to eliminate evil, some portions of the scriptures may be overlooked.

Through Jesus, we learnt that God's word can be refined for the good of mankind. By the law given through Moses, the woman caught in adultery was supposed to be stoned to death, but Jesus opened up our understanding – that any religion which lacks conscience, terrifies people, or make people commit sin in the name of correcting the wrong of others is ungodly. If a religion makes people to commit murder in the name of obeying God's word, such religion is not of God, but worldly religion. Jesus overlooked the written law of God on that day by putting compassion ahead of what was written. It thus teaches us that all godliness must tend towards the good of the people. Why would a godly soul witness people stoning another human being like themselves to death, talk-less of being a partaker of the crime? Can two wrongs make a right?

The German philosopher and economist, Karl Marx viewed that "religion is the opium of the people" and I tend to believe this in part. I believe it because in several communities, especially African, and among Arabs, there are sets of people who claim to have elevated access to God. In these communities, God has been positioned as an ally to some mortal being. These classified individuals work on the psyche of their followers to make them do what they want them to do. Among some sects, the adherents are used to perpetrate mass killing through suicide bombings or the planting of devilish instruments of destruction. In some, the adherents are used as puppets to accrue wealth unto the leaders. However it is used, this practice is unscriptural, it is an ungodly act and I believe it takes away the good inherent in religious fellowship. It suppresses individual as well as communal piety. It divorces godly conscience from religion. For people to be of sound mind, each of us must learn to read the scripture with a free mind. Not through the lenses that have been implanted in us, probably from infancy or through leaders who have their agenda. We must learn to know God for ourselves. Such move will bring about encouraging reformation of religions and the religious. Then each of us will be able to see God as being present in each other's chosen faith, and see Jesus the Messiah as the center of godliness.

Also from Tunji Oreyingbo …

TO SAVE THE FALLING NATIONS: A Physical Task for Spiritual Leaders

The nations of Africa are in a hopeless situation. Corruption in the continent is endemic, and has made the continent the poorest in the world. Dr. Tunji Oreyingbo teaches practical ways that African Spiritual leaders can help transform the continent into the pride of nations. Using Apostle Paul as a model pedagogue, he expounds on the Apostle's practical comport principles and how these principles, if followed by the African Church leaders will make them of great repute before the nations political leaders. These principles have potentials to propel gradual and continuous positive change in the entire continent of Africa.

www.ingramcontent.com/pod-product-compliance
Lightning Source LLC
Chambersburg PA
CBHW021429070526
44577CB00001B/135